First Choice

PUBLISHERS

Photography by
Lee Peterson

Text by
Don E. Shannon

Edited by
Lowell Lindsay

Art Direction by
Susan Burdick

SAN DIEGO • Copyright 1991 by First Choice Publishers
All Rights Reserved
Library of Congress Catalog Card Number 91-73732
ISBN 0-916251-45-4

Third Printing
Distributed by Sunbelt Publications, Inc.

Published in the United States of America
by First Choice Publishers
P.O. Box 191126
San Diego, CA 92159
Printed and Bound in Korea

Mission San Diego de Alcala.

The "Old Spanish Lighthouse" on Point Loma is neither really "old" nor "Spanish."
It was built in 1854, but was located too high and fog obscured its light. It was replaced later with
a more modern structure located nearer the water.

Il "Vecchio faro di San Diego" a Point Loma non è molto "vecchio" nè "spagnolo."
Fu costruito nel 1854, ma fu collocato troppo alto e la nebbia oscurava la sua luce. Fu sostituito più tardi con una
struttura più moderna situata vicino al mare.

"El viejo faro español" en Punta Loma no es ni tan "viejo" ni "español."
Se construyó en 1854, pero se colocó demasiado alto y la niebla ocultó su luz. Fué reemplazado después por
una estructura más moderna colocado más cerca al mar.

実際にはそれほど古くもスペイン風でもない、ポイント・ロマ岬の"Old Spanish Lighthouse"。
1854年の当初のライトハウスは非常に高い所に建てられ、霧のため光がぼやけ、
後年、海辺近くに近代的なデザインで再築された。

SAN DIEGO

PHOTOGRAPHY BY LEE PETERSON
TEXT BY DON E. SHANNON

SAN DIEGO

This place called San Diego has always been close to the edge of the world. Most of its human history has been spent in isolation, a condition dictated by its own geography. With arid deserts and rugged mountains to the south and east, overland travelers found no easy access to the region. The vastness of the Pacific Ocean provided San Diego with an equally daunting barrier to the west. This enforced solitude has given the area its distinct character, personality and flavor.

San Diego, like all hard-to-get-to places, has acquired a romance all its own: The Never-Never Land, the unknown that lies beyond the ranges, the impossible dream. Perhaps it has always been this way. Long ago, sometime in the mist-shrouded times of pre-history, the first human migrants reached San Diego. They were travel-hardened nomads who forged a passage from the Colorado River across the desert wastelands to the sea. For more than 10,000 years they, and later arrivals, were the lords and masters of the region and its only human occupants. Never numerous, their small villages were sheltered along streams and springs of fresh water. Over the millenniums little changed in their culture. While distant tribes developed sophisticated agricultural practices and built elaborate cities, these first San Diegans remained simple hunters and gatherers.

Less than five hundred years ago the barriers that hid the primitive Indian world began to crumble. A hint of the change came with the appearance in 1542 of a Spanish squadron probing the unknown reaches of the Paciifc. Their visit was brief, but San Diego's excellent bay was duly noted. A testimony to the isolation of the place is the fact that sixty years elapsed before the area was visited again, and more than two centuries passed before a permanent Hispanic settlement was established here. In the "Age of Sail" this place was one of the most distant from the busy worlds of Europe and the Atlantic. Adverse winds and currents made voyages to San Diego dangerous and difficult.

At first the colonists of the region huddled under the protection of the mission, presidio and pueblo. Their fields and pasture lands lay close to the banks of the river and they were content. Later, under Mexican rule,

expeditions explored the interior regions, crossing the mountains and marking routes to the East. By the 1820s a few frontiersmen and trappers from the United States had managed to penetrate the harsh deserts and reach San Diego overland. At the same time, intrepid Yankee captains brought their ships into the bay and began a lively trade in sea otter pelts and cattle hides. While the region was largely left out of the prosperity and growth caused by the great gold rush of 1849, it continued to slowly develop and even had a small gold rush of its own a generation later.

The last half of the 19th century was a time of self-searching for San Diego. Newly arrived residents and visitors enjoyed the benign climate, but saw little else to recommend the region.

Despite moving the town to a more appropriate location along the bayshore, the settlement remained at the periphery of international events. Hopes for a transcontinental railroad connection with the East were repeatedly dashed. However, the value of a strategically placed natural harbor located on the southwesternmost place in the nation was appreciated by military planners and the small city became a "navy town."

And so it remained through the first half of the 20th century as well. Only after the Second World War did tourism begin to rival the military as a contributor to the San Diego economy. The population boomed as other Americans discovered the pleasures of life along the "Sundown Sea" and the city and its suburbs mushroomed in the hills and valleys to the north and east. Networks of freeways replaced the old highways and a countywide trolley system went into operation. San Diego swelled to metropolitan stature and became one of the largest cities in the United States.

Nevertheless, as the region awaits the dawning of the 21st century, its citizens still see it as the special place it has always been. New residents and visitors alike refer to this city as their Pacific paradise — cooled by Pacific breezes during the summer and warmed by the same ocean during the short winter — San Diego sparkles in the brilliant western sunshine and continues to be ... **America's finest city.**

This weathered building, near the ranch house of Juan Jose Warner, may date to the 1840s
and the Mexican period in San Diego history.

La casa del Ranch di Juan Josè Warner, invecchiata dal tempo, risale al 1840
del periodo messicano della storia di San Diego.

La vieja casa desgastada del rancho de Juan José Warner fué construido en la década de 1840,
el periodo mexicano de San Diego.

Juan Jose Warner のひなびた牧場の家は、1840年代のサンディエゴ歴史における
メキシコ時代を象徴する。

SAN DIEGO

Este lugar llamado San Diego siempre ha estado cerca de la periferia del mundo. Gran parte de su historia humana se ha desenvuelto en aislamiento, una condición mandada por su propia geografía. Con desiertos áridos y montañas escarpadas al sur y al este, los viajeros terrestres no encontraron acceso fácil a la región. La inmensidad del Océano Pacífico dejó a San Diego con un obstáculo igualmente imponente al oeste. Esta soledad forzada ha dado al área su carácter distinto, personalidad y encanto.

San Diego como muchos lugares inaccesibles ha adquirido un carácter romántico único: la tierra de maravillas, lo desconocido que queda más allá de las cordilleras, el sueño imposible. Quizás siempre haya sido asi. Hace mucho tiempo, alguna vez en las tinieblas de la pre-historia, los primeros emigrados humanos llegaron a San Diego. Ellos eran nómadas toscos quienes forjaron un camino del Río Colorado por el desierto inhabitable hasta el mar. Por más de diez mil años ellos, y otros de aparición más tardía eran los señores y patrones de la región y sus únicos habitantes humanos. Nunca numerosos, sus pueblos pequeños fueron abrigados a la orilla de arroyos y manantiales de agua dulce. Por milenios su cultura se desarrolló poco mientras que tribus alejadas desarrollaron sistemas agrarias sofisticados y construyeron ciudades sumamente elaboradas; estos primeros Diegueños siguieron siendo sencillos cazadores y recolectores.

Hace menos de quinientos años las barreras que ocultaron el mundo indiano primitivo empezaron a derrumbarse. Una insinuación del cambio vino con la llegàda en 1542 de una escuadra española sondeando las orillas desconocidas del Pacífico. Su visita fué breve, pero la excelente bahía de San Diego fué debidamente registrada. Una prueba del aislamiento del lugar es que transcurrieron sesenta años hasta que el área fué visitada otra vez, y más de dos siglos pasaron antes de que una presencia hispana duradera fuera establecida. En el siglo de la exploración de las nuevas tierras este sitio se encontraba entre los lugares más distantes del turbulento mundo de Europa y el Atlántico. Vientos adversos y corrientes contrarios hacía del viaje a San Diego una empresa peligrosa y difícil.

Al principio los colonos de la región se ampararon bajo la protección de la misión, presidio y pueblo. Sus cultivos y pasturas bordeaban los bancos del río y los pobladores estaban a gusto. Más tarde, bajo el mando mexicano, varias expediciones

exploraron tierra adentro, cruzando las montañas y estableciendo rutas al este. Durante de la decada de 1820-1830 unos pocos pioneros y cazadores de los Estados Unidos lograron penetrar los desiertos ásperos y llegaron por tierra hasta San Diego. Al mismo tiempo, capitanes norteamericanos intrepidos arribaron sus barcos a la bahía y establecieron un comercio en pieles de nutria y cuero. A pesar de que la región quedaba en gran parte fuera de la prosperidad y crecimiento auspiciado por la fiebre de oro en 1849, siguió desarrollandose lentamente y hasta presenció su propia fiebre de oro pequeña una generación después.

La segunda mitad del siglo XIX fué una época de introspección para San Diego. Pobladores recién llegados así como visitantes gozaron del clima benigno, pero no encontraron mucho más que esto. A pesar de que se hubiera mudado el pueblo a un sitio más apropiado frente la bahía, el asentamiento quedó en la periferia de acontecimientos internacionales. Esperanzas de una vinculación ferroviaria transcontinental con el este fueron repetidamente truncados. Sin embargo, el valor de un puerto natural estratégicamente ubicado en el lugar más al suroeste del país fué apreciado por planificadores militares y la ciudad pequeña llegó a ser "un pueblo naval."

Así transcurrió la primera mitad del siglo XX. Inmediatamente después de la segunda guerra mundial la industria del turismo empezó a competir con las fuerzas armadas como principal contribuyente a la economia de San Diego. La población creció rápidamente cuando otros norteamericanos descubrieron los placeres de la vida frente las puestas del sol y la ciudad y sus suburbios proliferaron en las colinas y valles al norte y al este. Redes de autopistas reemplazaron los caminos viejos y un sistema de tranvía se estableció para el condado. San Diego alcanzó la condición de una metrópoli y llegó a ser una de las ciudades más grandes de los Estados Unidos.

No obstante, mientras que la región espera el amanecer del siglo XXI, sus ciudadanos todavía la ven como a tierra encantada que siempre ha sido. Tanto los nuevos residentes como aquellos que la visitan llaman a esta ciudad "el paraíso del Pacífico" — refrescado por las brisas del Pacífico durante el verano y calentado por el mismo océano durante el corto invierno — San Diego reluce bajo el brillante sol occidental y sigue siendo ... **"la ciudad más agradable de norteamerica."**

San Diego pioneer George Marston constructed and donated
the Junipero Serra Museum in Old Town to the city in 1929.

Il pioniere di San Diego, George Marston costruì e donò il Museo Junipero Serra,
nella Città Vecchia, alla città nel 1929.

El pionero diegueño George Marston construyó y donó el
Museo Junípero Serra en el Pueblo Viejo a la cuidad en 1929.

サンディエゴの開拓者である George Marston は、1929年にオールドタウンに
Junipero Serra 博物館を建造し、市に寄贈。

SAN DIEGO

Questo posto chiamato San Diego è sempre stato vicino al margine del mondo. Gran parte della sua storia umana è stata spesa in isolamento a condizioni imposte dalla sua posizione geografica. Con aridi deserti e aspre montagne al sud e ad est i viaggiatori per via di terra non avevano facile accesso alla regione. La vastità dell'Oceano Pacifico forniva a San Diego una, ugualmente intrepida barriera all'ovest. Questa rinforzata solitudine ha dato al luogo un distinto carattere, personalità e sapore.

San Diego come tutti i luoghi difficili da raggiungere, ha acquisito una sua propria storia romanzata "La terra del mai." L'ignoto che si nasconde aldilà dei limiti, il sogno impossibile. Forse è sempre stato così. Un tempo avvolto nelle nebbie della preistoria, i primi emigranti umani raggiunsero San Diego. Erano viaggiatori nomadi arditi che forzarono un passaggio dal Colorado River attraverso il desolato deserto, fino al mare. Per più di diecimila anni essi ed altri nuovi arrivati furono i signori e padroni della regione. I soli occupanti umani. Mai numerosi, i loro piccoli villaggi erano stazionati lungo corsi e sorgenti d'acqua fresca. Mentre lontane tribù sviluppavano sofisticati sistemi di agricoltura e costruivano elaborate città, insignificanti cambiamenti avvenivano nella cultura di San Diego e gli abitanti rimanevano semplici cacciatori e raccoglitori.

Meno di cinquecento anni fa le barriere che proteggevano il mondo dei primi indiani cominciarono a sgretolarsi. Un accenno di cambiamento arrivò con l'apparizione nel 1542 di uno squadrone spaghnolo che esplorava le nascoste ricchezze del Pacifico. La loro visita fu breve, ma l'eccellente baia di San Diego era ormai conosciuta. Una testimonianza dell'isolamento del posto è il fatto che trascorsero sessanta anni prima che la zona fosse visitata ancora. E più di due centenari trascorsero prima che un permanente insediamento spagnolo si stabilisse qui. Nell'"Età della Vela" questo posto era uno dei più distanti dall'attivo mondo dell'Europa e dell'Atlantico. I venti avversi e le correnti trasformavano i viaggi a San Diego in pericolosi e difficili.

All'zinizio i coloni della regione si accalcavano sotto la protezione della missione, del presidio e del pueblo. I loro campi e terre di pascolo erano vicine agli argini del fiume e gli abitanti erano soddisfatti.

Più tardi sotto le leggi Messicane, le spedizioni esplorarono l'interno delle regioni, attraversando le montagne e segnando i percorsi all'est. Nel 1820 alcuni pionieri e cacciatori dagli Stati Uniti riuscirono a penetrare l'arido deserto e a raggiungere la terra di San Diego. A medesimo tempo, intrepidi capitani Yankee spinsero le loro navi fino alla baia e iniziarono un vivace scambio sul mare di pelle di lontre e di bestiame. Sebbene la regione era in gran parte lasciata fuori dalla prosperità e crescita economica causata dalla corsa all'oro del 1849, essa continuava lentamente a svilupparsi ed ebbe anche una propria corsa all'oro una generazione più tardi.

L'ultima metà del secolo 1900 era un'epoca di autoricerca per San Diego. I nuovi arrivati, residenti e visitatori godevano del clima favorevole, ma avevano poco altro da apprezzare della regione. Anzichè spostare la città in un luogo più appropriato lungo il mare, lo stanziamento rimase dov'era e a causa di ciò rimase anche alla periferia degli eventi internazionali. Speranze per una connessione ferroviaria transcontinentale con l'est furono ripetitivamente distrutte. Tuttavia il valore di un posto strategicamente collocato in un porto naturale nel sud-ovest della Nazione era apprezzata da progettisti militari e la piccola città divenne una "città navale."

Così rimase anche durante tutta la prima metà del Ventesimo secolo. Solo dopo la prima Guerra Mondiale il turismo iniziò a rivaleggiare con i militari e a contribuire all'economia di San Diego. La popolazione esplose quando altri americani scoprsero il piacere della vita lungo "il mare del tramonto" e la città si sviluppò nelle valli e colline dal nord all'est. Un sistema di autostrade rimpiazzarono le vecchie strade pubbliche e un sistema locale di filobus, iniziò a operare. San Diego prese una statura metropolitana e divenne una delle città più grandi degli Stati Uniti.

Ciò monostante aspettando gli albori del ventesimo secolo, la regione continua ad essere riconosciuta dai suoi abitanti come quel posto speciale che è sempre stato. Nuovi abitanti e visitatori parlano di questa città come del loro Pacifico paradiso, rinfrescato dalla brezza del Pacifico durante l'estate e riscaldato dallo stesso oceano durante il breve inverno. San Diego splende nel brillante sole dell'ovest e continua ad essere ... **"la più bella città americana."**

The Santa Ysabel Asistencia was a sub-mission established by Spanish Franciscan fathers in 1816.

La Santa Ysabel Asistencia era una sotto-missione fondata dai frati Fracescani spagnoli nel 1816.

La Asistencia de Santa Ysabel fué una doctrina establecida por frailes franciscanos españoles en 1816.

Santa Ysabel Asistenciaは、1816年にスペインの聖フランチェスコの神父達により設立された下位修道所。

SAN DIEGO

常に世界のはずれ近くに位置してきたサンディエゴ。そしてそこに住む人々の歴史は、その地理的な条件の為孤立したものであった。乾ききった荒野、南から東へと伸びる険しい山々の為、陸路を旅する人々にとって、この地に踏みいるのは容易なことではなかった。又、広大な太平洋は西方への障壁となっていた。こういった地理的条件に強いられた孤立は、サンディエゴという地に、他とは異なった独特な特性、味わいを与えた。

容易には到達できないすべての場所がそうであるように、サンディエゴはそこだけにしかないロマンを感じさせる: 遠くめったに人が行かない〝ネバーネバーランド〟、未知の領域、不可能な夢といった……
先史時代の霧に包まれた大昔に、最初の移住者達がサンディエゴにたどり着いた。彼等は荒野を横切り、コロラドリバーからの道を押し進んできた遊牧民であった。それからの1万年以上の間、この最初の移住民とその後続者達は、まさにこの地の所有者であり、支配者であった──唯一の人間居住者。彼等は川の支流や湧き水の出るほとりに村をなし、ひっそりと暮らしていた。遠く離れた地に住む民族が新しい農作方法をあみだしたり、町造りをしている一方、この地の住民は狩猟などの極めて簡素な生活様式を守っていた。

500年足らず以前に、この原始的なインディアンの世界を覆い隠していた障壁が崩れ始めた。このきっかけとなったのは、1542年の太平洋の未開地を探検していたスペイン艦隊の出現であった。逗留は短かったものの、サンディエゴ湾の素晴らしさは、しっかりと彼等の脳裏に焼き付いた。しかし、再びこの地に人が足を踏み入れるまでに60年が経過し、更にラテン系民族が定住するまでには2世紀が過ぎた。それはとりもなおさず、この地がそれだけ孤立していたという証である。「Age of Sail─航海時代」において、この地はヨーロッパや大西洋諸国のあわただしい世界から最も離れていた。逆風や逆流が、サンディエゴへの航海を危険かつ困難なものにしていたからである。

当初、植民地住民は修道所、要塞地や石造りの住居部落の防護のもとに群集まっていた。田畑や牧草地は河岸に近く、彼等の生活は充足していた。その後メキシコ支配下にある時、探検隊が山を越え道しるべをつけながら内陸を探検した。1820年代までには、アメリカ本土から数人の辺境開拓者や猟師が苛酷な旅を克服し、サンディエゴに辿りついた。同じ頃、勇猛なアメリカ人船長がサンディエゴ湾に上陸し、ラッコの毛皮や牛皮などの商売を始めた。1849年のゴールドラッシュによる好景気には大きく取り残されたが、この地の発展への歩みはゆっくりではあるが止まることなく進み、1世代後には小規模なゴールドラッシュさえ迎えた。

19世紀の後半はサンディエゴにとって〝自己再吟味〟の時期であった。新参者はこの温和な気候を楽しんだが、その他にはこれといったものがなかった。湾岸に町を移したものの、まだ国際的行事の外側に置かれていた。東部との接続のための大陸横断鉄道の夢は、幾度も打ち砕かれてしまった。しかし、西南の最端に位置する天然の良港は海軍基地として最適であり、この小さな町は〝海軍の町〟として栄えた。

20世紀前半は海軍の町のままであったが、第2次世界大戦後には、観光事業が海軍基地に代わって、サンディエゴの経済に貢献するようになった。他のアメリカ人達が太平洋に沈む夕日の美しさに酔いしれ、素晴らしさを実感するようになると、市中や郊外の住宅建設が急速に進み、人口は急激に増加した。古い幹線道路に取って替わり、フリーウェイが縦横に走り、カウンティ全体には路面電車が運行された。こうして、サンディエゴは主要都市として発展し、アメリカ全土でも最大都市のひとつとなった。

しかし、このように発展し、21世紀の幕開けを間近にした現在でも、サンディエゴの住人にとって、サンディエゴとはずっとそうであったように、他とは違う特別な所なのである。新しく移り住んできた人も、ひとときの観光に訪れる人も、口を揃えて〝ここサンディエゴは太平洋のパラダイス〟と賞する……雄大な太平洋から夏には涼風、そして短い冬の間には暖かな風……。
サンディエゴは、アメリカの最高の都市として西の青空に、今日もきらめいている。

The observatory at Mount Palomar, completed in 1948, is still in use by astronomers
and is considered one of the finest facilities of its kind in the world.

L'osservatorio del Monte Palomar, completato nel 1948, è tuttora usato dagli astronomi
ed è considerato uno dei più rinomati servizi del suo genere nel mondo.

El observatorio del Cerro Palomar, terminado en 1948, es todavía usado por astrónomos y es considerado uno
de los mejores de su clase en el mundo.

1948年に完成されたパロマー山の天文台は、今なお天文学者に利用され、
世界最大級の反射望遠鏡を備えた天文台である。

Rural mailboxes near Ramona provide a pastoral setting to the countryside.

Cassette postali in zone rurali vicino a Ramona creano uno scenario pastorale nella campagna.

Buzones rurales cerca de Ramona prestan un ambiente pastoral al campo.

Ramona近郊の田舎の郵便ポスト。

A view across the apple orchards of Julian to the rugged Vulcan Mountains to the east.

Una vista attraverso i frutteti di meli di Julian fino alle montagne ad est.

Una vista por los manzanares de Julían hacía las ásperas Monontañas Volcanes al este.

ジュリアンのりんご園から東にのびる険しい山並。

Indian petroglyphs are found in some of the more remote parts of the San Diego back country.

Petroglifici indiani sono stati trovati in alcune delle più remote zone nell'entroterra di S.Diego.

Petroglifos indios se encuentran en algunas de las partes más apartadas del campo de San Diego.

辺鄙な田園地方に行くと、インディアンの岩面彫刻を目にする。

The early morning winter sun provides scant warmth for these horses in a corral near Poway.

Il sole del primo mattino invernale fornisce un flebile calore a questi cavalli nel recinto, vicino a Poway.

El sol mañanero de invierno proporciona poco calor para estos caballos en un corral cerca de Poway.

冬の早朝の光が、Poway付近の柵囲いの馬にやわらかな日差しを投げかける。

Low tides and nearly flat beaches mirror distant buildings and sky.

La bassa marea e spiagge quasi piatte rispecchiano i lontani palazzi e il cielo.

Mareas bajas y playas casí planas reflejan edificios distantes y el cielo.

ほとんど波のないビーチに、遠くのビルや空が映し出される。

The Hotel Del Coronado, originally constructed in 1888, remains a landmark of another era.

L'Hotel Del Coronado, originariamente costruito nel 1888, rimane una pietra miliare di un'altra epoca.

El Hotel Del Coronado, originalmente construído en 1888, sigue siendo un lugar destacado de otra era.

1888年に建造されたHotel Del Coronadoは、ひとつの時代を代表する名ホテル。

The "El Cortez," once a prominent hotel and early San Diego landmark,
reflects in the glass of a modern office building.

"El Cortez," una volta un prominente hotel e antica pietra miliare di San Diego
si riflette nel vetro di un moderno edificio commerciale.

"El Cortez," una vez un hotel prominente y uno de los edificios más reconocidos de San Diego,
reflejado en los vidrios de un edificio comercial moderno.

近代オフィスビルの硝子にうつる、かつての有名なホテルであり昔のサンディエゴの
ランドマーク "El Cortez"。

San Diego as seen from Point Loma looking east to the mountainous interior.

San Diego vista da Point Loma, guardando ad est verso l'entroterra montagnoso.

San Diego y el interior montañoso visto desde Punta Loma.

ポイント・ロマから一望するサンディエゴ。

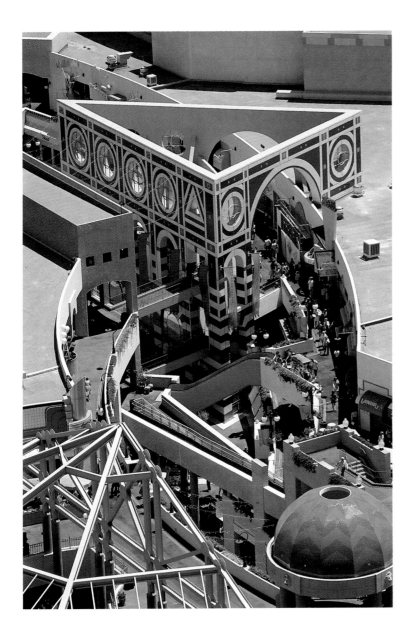

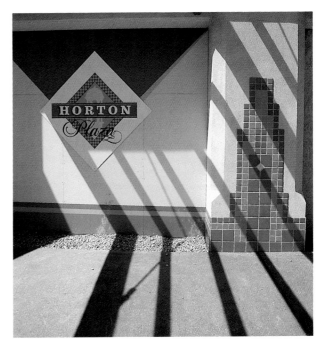

An important part of the renaissance of downtown was the completion of the
Horton Plaza Shopping Center with its circus-like mix of colors and architecture.

Una parte importane della rinascita del centro città fu il completamento della piazza
Horton-Centro Commerciale, simile a un circo pieno di colori e architettura.

Una faceta importante del renacimiento del centro urbano fué la construcción del centro comercial
Horton Plaza que parece un circo con su mezcla de colores pintorescos y arquitectura extravegante.

ダウンタウンの復興に大きな役割を果たしたのは、色と建築のサーカスのような構造の
Horton Plaza Shopping Center の完成である。

San Diego's skyline and bold new architecture emulate the enduring palm tree.

Il profilo di s.Diego e l'audace architettura emulano la durevole palma.

La perspectiva de San Diego y su nueva arquitectura audaz, emulan a la perdurable palmera.

パーム・ツリーと競うようこそびえる斬新なデザインのサンディエゴの新しいビル群。

With a waterfront setting on the harbor and a sail-like roof, the new Convention Center
is the hub of downtown San Diego.

Con il lungomare nel porto e un tetto "a vela," il nuovo Centro dei Congressi
è il fulcro della zona sud di San Diego.

Frente la bahía, con su techo en forma, de vela, el nuevo Centro de Convenciones es la
construcción más sobresaliente del centro de San Diego.

ハーバーの水面に、屋根が船の帆のようにつきだして建っている新しいコンベンションセンターは、
サンディエゴの中心である。

24

The University of California's Library, surrounded by eucalyptus trees,
is the architectural centerpiece of the campus.

La biblioteca dell'universitá di California circondata da acberi di eucaliptus, è
il pezzo architettonico centrale del campus.

La biblioteca de la Universidad de California, rodeada por eucaliptos,
es su edificio más sobresaliente.

周囲をユーカリの木で囲まれるように建つカリフォルニア大学の図書館は、
その独特のデザインでキャンパスのシンボルとされています。

Sea World of San Diego provides exciting attractions for all ages.

Il Mondo Marino (Sea World) di San Diego fornisce attrazioni emozionanti a tutte le età.

Sea World (el Mundo Marítimo) de San Diego proporciona atraciones emocionantes
para gente de todas edades.

シーワールドでは様々なエキサイティングなショーを網羅しており、
年齢を問わず誰もが楽しめる。

26

The Mission Beach "Coaster," carefully restored after years of disuse, rides again.

La Mission Beach "Coaster," accuratamente ristrutturata dopo anni di abbandono, funziona ancora.

La montaña rusa de Playa Misión cuidadosamente restaurada después
de años de abandono; corre de nuevo.

長い間使われていなかったミッションビーチのジェットコースターも、慎重に修復され、
再び運転されている。

Balboa Park, the Jewel of the City, was set aside over 100 years ago for the enjoyment of San Diegans
Early development took place for the California-Panama exhibition of 1915, and established a legacy
of unique architecture, ponds, and fountains.

Balboa Park, il gioiello della città fu studiato più di cento anni fa in particolare per il piacere
dei Sandiegani. Un primo sviluppo iniziò con la mostra California-Panama del 1915, e lasciò in
eredità un'architettura unica, laghetti e fontane.

El Parque Balboa, la joya de la ciudad, fué apartado hace más de cien años por el placer de los ciudadanos.
El desenvolvimiento temprano tuvo lugar para la exhibición de California-Panamá en 1915, y se estableció
una herencia de arquitectura única, estanques y fuentes.

サンディエゴ市の宝石ともいうべきバルボア公園は、100年以上も前は、サンディエゴ市民のみに楽しま
れていたが、1915年にはカリフォルニア—パナマ博覧会の会場にもなり、文化活動の中心となっている。
ユニークな建物、池、噴水等がそのまま残っている。

Fort Rosecrans National Cemetery occupies a portion of Point Loma
and enjoys a panoramic view of the city and bay.

Il Cimitero Nazionale di Fort Rosecrans occupa una parte di Point Loma
e gode di una vista panoramica della città e della baia.

El cementerio nacional del fuerte Rosecrans ocupa una porción de Punta Loma
y goza de una vista panorámica de la ciudad y la bahía.

Fort Rosecrans国立墓地はポイント・ロマ岬の一角にあり、そこからは
サンディエゴ市街や湾の素晴らしい景観が一望できる。

The "new" and still active Point Loma Lighthouse.

Il "nuovo" e tuttora attivo faro di Point Loma.

El "nuevo" y aún activo faro de Punta Loma.

今なお利用されている"新しい"ポイント・ロマ岬のライトハウス

The San Diego-Coronado Bay Bridge replaced ferry service for thousands of motorists,
and was completed in 1969.

Il Ponte San Diego-Coronado sostituisce il servizio di traghetto per migliaia
di motoristi e fu completato nel 1969.

El Puente de San Diego-Coronado Bay reemplazó el servicio de transbordador por miles de conductores.
Se terminó de construir en 1969.

それまでのフェリーに取って替わる、サンディエゴ ——コロナード・ベイブリッジが
1969年に完成された。

Opened in October, 1991, Loew's Coronado Bay Resort exemplifies the
new style of luxury hotels offering relaxation to visitors.

Aperto ad Ottobre 1991, Loew's Coronado Bay Resort, mostra il nuovo
concetto d'alberghi di lusso per il riposo dei visitatori.

Inaugurado en octubre de 1991, Loew's Coronado Bay Resort
demuestra el nuevo estilo en hoteles de lujo que
ofrecen relajamiento a sus visitantes.

1991年10月のオープン以来、ロウズ・コロナド・ベイ・リゾートは
旅行者がくつろげる高級ホテルの新しい姿を示し続けて来ました。

The sport fishing fleet offers year-round fishing off the coast of Southern California and Mexico.

I battelli per le sport della pesca offrono pesca tutto l'anno lungo la costa al
largo del sud della California e del Messico.

La flota pesquera ofrece pesca deportiva todo el año por la costa del sur de California y Mexico.

南カリフォルニアやメキシコ沿岸では、スポーツフィッシングが１年中楽しめる。

Sailing to Pacific destinations, both near and far, is an exciting part of San Diego's waterfront.

Navigare nel Pacifico per destinazioni sia vicine che lontane è
un'eccitante aspetto del lungomare di San Diego.

Navegando por el Pacífico destinos cercanos y lejanos, es una parte fascinante del puerto de San Diego.

近距離でも遠距離でも、エキサイティングな太平洋のセーリングが楽しめる。

The Berkeley, an 1898 San Francisco ferry boat and the Medea, 1904 steam yacht
are part of the Maritime Museum at the San Diego harborside.

Il Berkeley, un ferry boat di S.Francisco del 1898, e la Medea, uno yacht a
vapore del 1904, fanno parte del Museo Marittimo al porto di San Diego.

El Berkeley, un transbordador de San Francisco de 1898 y el Medea, un yate de vapor de 1904
forman parte del Museo Marítimo del puerto de San Diego.

サンディエゴ港のふちには海洋博物館として、1898年製サンフランシスコのフェリーポート、
バークレイ号と1904年製の蒸気ヨット、メディア号が保存されている。

The Star of India, the oldest iron sailing ship in the world, still sails
in San Diego as part of the Maritime Museum.

La Stella dell'India, la più antica nave a vela in ferro esistente al mondo,
tuttora naviga a S.Diego come parte del Museo Marittimo.

La Estrella de India, el barco de vela de construcción de hierro más antiguo en el mundo,
todavía se encuentra en San Diego como parte del Museo Marítimo.

現存する鉄製帆船では世界最古の、スター・オブ・インディア号が
海洋博物館として係留されている。

Informal "beer can races" are held on summer evenings on San Diego Bay.

Informali "gare di birra" si tengono nelle serate estive nella baia a San Diego.

Informales "carreras de latas de cerveza" se ven en las noches de verano en la Bahía de San Diego.

サンディエゴ湾で夏の夜に開かれる "ビールの空きかん競争"

The new International America's Cup Class boats prepare for the America's Cup races.

La nuova classe per la Coppa Internazionale Americana si prepara per la gara della Coppa Americana.

Los barcos de la nueva clase de la Copa Internacional de América se preparan para
la competencia de la Copa de América.

アメリカ・カップレースに向けて準備中の、新インターナショナル・アメリカ・カップ・クラスのボート。

A sea lion sunning himself on a harbor buoy does his best
to ignore a sailboat passing close to his perch.

Una foca si riscalda al sole in una boa-salvagente nel porto e fa del suo meglio per
ignorare una barca a vela che passa vicino al suo posto di ristoro.

Una foca se asolea en una boya de la bahía y trata de pasar por alto a un barco de
vela que pasa cerca de su percha.

近づくセールボートを無視しながら、ハーバーに浮かぶブイで、
日光浴をしているアザラシ。

The aircraft carrier Kitty Hawk, with the crew "manning the rails," arrives in San Diego Bay.

Il corriere aereo Kitty Hawk con l'equipaggio schierato in parata, entra nel porto di San Diego.

El portaaviones Kitty Hawk, con su tripulación, arriba en la Bahía de San Diego.

サンディエゴ湾に入港した空母キティホークと乗組員。

San Diego in evening glow.

San Diego nei bagliori della sera.

San Diego de noche.

夕日に染まるサンディエゴ。

Torrey Pines State Reserve boasts a unique tree, the Torrey Pine, as well as spectacular coastline.

Il Parco Statale di Torrey Pines vanta un albero raro, il Torrey Pine, come anche una costa spettacolare.

El Parque Estatal de Torrey Pines se alaba un árbol único, el Pino Torrey,
tanto como una costa espectácular.

Torrey Pines 州立公園は、珍しい樹木 Torrey Pine と美しい海岸線を誇っている。

Looking across San Diego Bay to Point Loma and the Springtime fog that lies just offshore.

Guardando lungo la Baia di S.Diego fino a Point Loma dove la nebbia primaverile si stende al largo.

El panorama por la Bahía de San Diego, Punta Loma y la niebla de primavera sobre la costa.

サンディエゴ湾からポイント・ロマにかけての眺めと春季の霧に煙る沖合い。

A landmark of the famous Scripps Institution of Oceanography
is its distinct pier buffeted here by winter storm surf.

Il famoso punto di confine dell'Istituto di Oceanografia è il suo distinto pontile colpito,
qui, dalle onde della risacca invernale.

Una imagen muy conocida del famoso Instituto de Oceanografía Scripps es el muelie distinto,
aquí golpeado por las olas de una tormenta invernal.

この荒波にもまれた桟橋こそ、有名なScripps海洋学会の
ランドマークである。

Lake Hodges, a major reservoir for water storage, overflows during winter rains.

Il Lago Hodges, un grande bacino idrico per la riserva d'acqua, straripa durante le piogge invernali.

El Lago Hodges, una alberca mayor de agua potable, rebosa bajo las lluvias del invierno.

主要な貯水池であるレイク・ホッジズは、冬季には雨で湖の水が溢れる。

Children play on the sand in Mission Beach.

I bambini giocanno nella sabbia a Mission Beach.

Niños jugando en la arena en Mission Beach.

ミッションビーチの砂浜で遊ぶ子供たち。

Seals bask in the sun along the La Jolla seawall.

Le foche si sdragiano sotto il solle
sulla costa di La Jolla.

Focas tomando el sol a lo largo del dique de La Jolla.

ラホヤの防波堤に乗って日光浴をするアザラシ。

The colossal power of a wave at La Jolla Cove hurtles surfers forward at awesome speeds, while the gentle breezes from the Pacific ocean meet the high cliffs of Torrey Pines providing ideal conditions for the sport of hang gliding.

La forte potenza di un'onda nell'insenatura di La Jolla scaglia i surfisti ad una imponente velocità, mentre la gentile brezza del'Oceano Pacifico si incontra con le alte vette di Torrey Pines fornendo condizioni ideali per lo sport del deltaplano.

La fuerza colosal de una ola en la caleta de La Jolla arroja surfeadores a una tremenda velocidad, mientras que las brisas suaves del Océano Pacífico encuentran las escarpaduras altas de Torrey Pines proporcionando perfectas condiciones para el deporte de hang-gliding (planear de mano).

ラ・ホヤ　コーブ（入り江）の波は猛スピードでサーファーを運び、一方、
太平洋からゆるやかに吹く風はTorrey Pinesの崖へぶつかり、
ハングライディングにとって絶好の風となる。

A diver explores the wonders of Scripps Canyon at the
Marine Underwater Park off the shores of La Jolla.

Un subacqueo esplora le meraviglie dello Scripps Canyon al Parco
sottomarino al largo di La Jolla.

Un buceador explora las maravillas del Cañon de Scripps
en el Parque Submarino frente las playas de La Jolla.

ラ・ホヤ沖合いの海底公園、Scripps Canyon の海底の驚異を探検するダイバー。

Colorful Nudibranch and eggs.

Nudibranch colorati e uova.

Un Nudibranquiano pintoresco y sus huevos.

色彩の美しいアオウミウシと卵。

Del Mar Racetrack, the scene of many colorful activities such as the annual Fair,
hot air ballooning competition, and Thoroughbred Racing.

La Gara dei cavalli di Del Mar, una delle tante coloratissime attività, come quella della Fiera annuale,
gare di palloni ad aria calda e gare di purosangue.

El Hipódromo Del Mar, el lugar de muchas actividades pintorescas como la feria anual,
competencias de globos de aire caliente, y carreras de caballos de raza.

デルマー競馬場ではアニュアル・フェア、気球大会、そしてサラブレッド競馬など、
色々な催しが開かれる。

The glow of sunset from Ocean Beach.

I bagliori del tramonto dalla Ocean Beach.

La puesta del sol de la Playa Océano.

太平洋に沈む夕日。

Sunset and clouds add drama to this view off Torrey Pines.

Il tramonto e le nuvole drammatizzano ancora di
piu questa vista di Torrey Pines.

La puesta del sol y las nubes le dan drama
a esta vista de Torrey Pines.

トーレイ・パインズから見たドラマチックな夕日と雲。

Mission Bay, yet another San Diego playground, grew from tidal flats and
the foresight of citizens after World War II.

La Mission Bay, ancora un altro luogo di ricreazione creato dalla bassa marea
e dalla previdenza dei cittadini dopo la II Guerra Mondiale.

Bahía Misión aún otro lugar de recreo en San Diego, fué reclamado del mar gracias a la
previsión de algunos ciudadanos después de la segunda guerra mundial.

サンディエゴのプレイグラウンド、ミッション・ベイは干潟から造られたもので、
第２次世界大戦後のサンディエゴ市民の先見の明といえよう。

A replica of Sir Francis Drake's Golden Hind came to San Diego. In 1579 the original ship
stopped on the California coast en route to the first English circumnavigation of the world.

Una riproduzione della Sir Francis Drake's Golden Hind arrivò a San Diego. Nel 1579 la nave originale
si fermò nella Costa Californiana sulla via verso la prima circumnavigazione inglese del mondo.

Una réplica del Golden Hind de Sir Francis Drake vino a San Diego. En 1579 el pirata inglés
llegó a la costa californiana. En este viaje Drake fué el primer inglés que circumnavigó al globo.

地球を周航した最初のイギリス人が、周航途中にカリフォルニア沿岸に寄港したのは1579年。
イギリス人提督の"Golden Hind"号の複製。

PLEASE DO NOT
ANNOY, TORMENT,
PESTER, PLAGUE,
MOLEST, WORRY,
BADGER, HARRY,
HARASS, HECKLE,
PERSECUTE, IRK,
BULLYRAG, VEX,
DISQUIET, GRATE,
BESET, BOTHER,
TEASE, NETTLE,
TANTALIZE, OR
RUFFLE THE ANIMALS

San Diego's world famous Zoo and Wild Animal Park have been on the forefront
of endangered species breeding and preservation programs.

Il famoso Zoo Mondiale di S.Diego e il Parco degli animali selvaggi sono stati parte centrale di attività
per la protezione delle speci animali in pericolo di estinzione e dei programmi per la loro conservazione.

El famoso Zoológico de San Diego y el Parque de Animales Silvestres han sido
en el primer lugar de la crianza y preservación de fauna en peligro de extinguirse.

世界的に有名なサンディエゴ動物園と野性動物公園は、絶滅寸前の生物の繁殖と
保護プログラム活動の中心となっている。

Dolphins play in the waves along the coast.

Delfini giocano nelle onde lungo la costa.

Delfines juegan en las olas costeñas.

波とたわむれるイルカ。

Under the waves swim a mother whale and her calf.

Sotto le onde nuotano le balene.

Una ballena y su ballenato nadan debajo las olas.

波の下で泳ぐ鯨の母子。

Giant kelp in its natural environment just off San Diego's coastline . . .
and washed ashore under brilliant sunshine.

Alghe giganti nel loro ambiente naturale al largo della costa di San Diego . . .
e la riva bagnata sotto un sole splendente.

Algas gigantescas en su ambiente natural frente a la costa diegueña . . .
arrojadas a la playa bajo un sol brillante.

巨大な海藻……岸に打ち上げられ、陽光に照らされる海藻。

65

Agriculture is a major part of San Diego's economy, featuring Flowers, Avocados and Citrus.

L'agricoltura ha un ruolo di maggiore importanza nell'economia di S.Diego, produzione principale sono i fiori, Avodado e Agrumi.

Agricultura juega un papel importante en la economía de San Diego, destacando las flores, aguacates y frutas cítricas.

花、アボカドや柑橘類などの農業は、サンディエゴ経済の主役である。

It is difficult, at any age, to resist the beauty of acres of colorful ranunculus.

E' difficile, a qualsiasi età, resistere alla bellezza di distese di ranuncoli coloratissimi.

Es difícil, no importa su edad, resistir la belleza de hectárias de rananculos pintorescos.

一面に咲く色とりどりのキンポウゲ、その美しさには誰もが圧倒される。

The unusual Jacumba house commands a spectacular view over the Anza-Borrego desert.

L'insolita casa Jacumba domina una spettacolare vista sul deserto Anza-Borrego.

La insólita Casa Jacumba ofrece una vista espléndida del Desierto Anza-Borrego.

Anza-Borrego砂漠の素晴らしい景色を見下ろす、一風変わったJacumbaの家。

Ocotillo and Barrel Cactus, flower during a short springtime season in the Anza-Borrego Desert.

Ocotillo e Barrel Cactus, fioriscono durante una breve primavera nel deserto Anza-Borrego.

Los cactos Ocotillo y Barril enflorecen durante la corta primavera del Desierto Anza-Borrego.

Anza-Borrego砂漠のタマサボテンなど、短い春の景色。

Sand in the desert beyond the mountains create a Sahara-like region rippled by the wind.

Sabbia nel deserto dietro le montagne crea un paesaggio simile al Sahara con ondulazioni create dal vento.

Arena en el desierto, más allá de las montañas, crea una región parecida a el Sáhara ondeada por el viento.

山々の向こうに、まるでサハラ砂漠のような波状になった砂丘。

Colorful cactus-like Euphorbs in Balboa Park.

Colorato deserto di Cactus a Balboa Park.

Cacto pintoresco en el Parque Balboa.

バルボア公園の色とりどりのサボテン。

The hot summers and dry hillsides are often scenes of brush fires such as this near Rancho Santa Fe.

Nelle calde estati gli aridi pendii dei colli sono spesso scena di incendi di
arbusti come questo vicino al Rancho Santa Fe.

Los veranos calientes y las colinas secas son muchas veces escenas
de incendios come este cerca de Rancho Santa Fé.

暑い夏には、Rancho Santa Fe近くの乾ききった山腹で、小さな山火事がおこる。

In mid-summer great thunderheads boil over the mountains and rise
thousands of feet above the Anza-Borrego Desert.

*A mezza estate grandi tuoni e nuvole 'ribolliscono' sopra le montagne
e salgono migliaia di metri sopra il Deserto Anza-Borrego.*

*Los grandes nubarrónes del verano sobre las montañas,
suben miles de pies sobre el Desierto Anza-Borrego.*

夏半ばには山々の頂に積乱雲が、Anza-Borrego 砂漠から
何千フィート高くまで湧き上がる。

Fog obscures the sea between Point Loma and Los Coronados,
four small islands off the coast of Mexico near the U.S. border.

Le nebbie oscurano il mare tra Point Loma e Los Coronados, quattro piccole
isole al largo della costa del Messico vicino il confine con gli Stati Uniti.

Niebla oculta el mar entre Punta Loma y las cuatro pequeñas Islas Coronados, en la costa fronteriza.

海からの霧で霞んで見えるポイント・ロマとロス・コロナード間の、
国境に近いメキシコ沿岸に浮かぶ小さな４つの島々。

Evening colors on Los Penasquitos Marsh near the coastline.

I colori della sera nella Los Penasquitos Marsh vicino la linea costiera.

La noche hermosa en la Ciénega Los Peñasquitos cerca del mar.

海岸線近くのLos Penasquitos湿地帯の夕焼け。

Surf fishing is a peaceful endeavor along miles of beaches.

La pesca nella risacca è una pacifica sfida nelle lunghe spiagge.

Pesca dentro del oleaje es un esfuerzo tranquilo por las extensas playas.

何マイルも続くビーチ沿いの、ほのぼのとしたウミタナゴ釣り。

Every mid-winter the ocean off the coast is the scene of the southern migration of the
Pacific Gray Whales. Their spouts can even be seen from shore as they swim
south to calve in the remote bays of Baja California.

Ogni metà inverno l'oceano al largo della costa è la scena della migrazione verso sud delle Balene Grigie
del Pacifico. Il loro zampillo può essere visto anche dalla riva mentre nuotano a sud per
andare a partorire nelle remote baie della Baia Californiana.

En pleno invierno el océano costeño es testigo a la migración al sur de las ballenas grises del Pacífico.
Se puede ver sus chorros desde la playa mientras que viajan a las bahías aisladas
de Baja California a parir.

毎年冬半ばに見られる、ヒゲ鯨の南への移動風景。お産のため遥か彼方のバハ、カリフォルニアへと、
泳ぎ渡っていく鯨達の吹く潮が沿岸からも見える。

The sunset silhouettes Crystal Pier, at Pacific Beach, on a winter evening.

Il tramonto disegna la silhouette di Crystal Pier, a Pacific Beach, in una sera invernale.

La puesta del sol detrás del Muelle Cristal, en la Playa Pacífico, en una noche de invierno.

冬の夕空に映し出される、クリスタル桟橋のシルエット。